# OLD RETFORD

*by*
David Ottewell

The Market Place at Retford prior to 1908 when the Angel Inn was adapted to provide offices for Henry Spencer's auctioneers business. Each Saturday in the early years of the twentieth century, Mr Spencer would conduct livestock auctions in the Market Place. The lamp standard surrounded by a chain fence became the site of the town's war memorial in the 1920s.

ISBN 1 84033 156 9

**FURTHER READING**

The books listed below were used by the author during his research. None of them are available from Stenlake Publishing. Those interested in finding out more are advised to contact their local bookshop or reference library.

Abelson, E. L., *Retford in Times Past*, Retford and District Historical and Archaeological Society, 1983.

Biggs B. J., *Looking at Old Retford*, Eaton Hall, 1968.

Biggs B. J., *The Methodists of Retford and District*, Retford Methodist Circuit, 1970.

Ed. Dolby M. et al, *Views of Old Retford*, Retford and District Historical and Archaeological Society, 1990.

Franks A. and G., *Retford on Old Picture Postcards*, Reflections, 1993.

Jackson A., *A History of Retford*, Eaton Hall, 1971.

Pirrcy J. S., *The History of Retford*, first published 1825, reprinted by Nottinghamshire County Council, 1994.

Roffey J., *The Book of Retford*, Barracuda, 1991.

Fletcher & Sons were based on Carolgate close to its junction with the Market Place. They were the leading drapers and furniture dealers in Retford and their catchphrase in the local newspaper was 'The house for value and variety'. In 1944 these premises were bought by the local co-operative society and renamed Centenary House. They were rebuilt in 1959, and when the shop reopened in August the following year it was called Co-operative House.

# INTRODUCTION

Retford's origins are lost in the mists of time, although it is known that there was a small settlement on the western bank of the River Idle prior to the Norman invasion of 1066. In the Domesday Book (1086), which detailed the extent of William the Conqueror's new kingdom, this is referred to as 'Redforde'. The name is thought to be derived from its situation at a crossing point of the River Idle where heavy red clay was visible at the surface.

From Norman times onwards a rival settlement grew up on the opposite bank of the river. To distinguish between the two the old village was deemed to be West Retford, and its upstart neighbour East Retford. The two settlements were distinctly separate from the outset, being run independently and soon having their own parish churches. East Retford was formally recognised about 1105 when Henry I created it a royal borough with permission to collect tolls from travellers crossing the River Idle.

East Retford grew quicker than its neighbour, and its importance was reaffirmed in 1246 when Henry III granted it a charter which, amongst other things, allowed it to hold an annual fair commencing on 31 May and lasting for eight days. The year 1279 saw the granting of a second charter, this time from Edward I. A clause permitting the holding of a market each Saturday established East Retford as the market centre for the surrounding countryside.

These charters, which could be renewed annually, were important as they brought a degree of self government to the town. In 1315 East Retford was allowed to send two representatives to King Edward's parliament in Lincoln. The first town hall was built in 1388 and, although only a wooden structure, it was a symbol of the wealth and importance of the town. The earliest surviving charter dates from 1313.

East Retford continued to develop and by the sixteenth century was allowed to hold three fairs, each four days long, annually. The town suffered a blow in 1528, when many of its wooden buildings were destroyed in a major fire, but it was only a temporary setback and in 1551 King Edward VI granted the town permission to establish a grammar school. In 1607 the first Stuart king, James I, granted East Retford a charter which allowed the town 'free' status and set out rules for its self government by a local council. At the same time East Retford was permitted to have its own coat of arms and a design involving a pair of falcons was selected.

Although by this time East Retford held a prominent position in the life of north Nottinghamshire, there were some significant developments in the eighteenth century that added to the town's status. In 1776 the Great North Road, linking London with Scotland, was diverted through Retford providing improved north–south communications and bringing visitors and trade to the area. During the following decade the Chesterfield Canal was routed from Worksop through Retford providing an east–west communication link. Both these developments made it easier to transport goods to and from the area, and East Retford became a natural point for travellers to break their journey. In the second half of the eighteenth century the centre of the town was redeveloped, with the market area moved from its traditional position in front of the parish church to a new site. This is still fronted by a number of Georgian and Victorian buildings.

The nineteenth century saw the arrival of the railways with the Manchester, Sheffield and Lincolnshire Company bringing their line through the town in 1849, to be followed by the Great Northern Railway later the same year. Again this made it easier for people to reach Retford and provided another means of transporting goods. The railways led to an increase in opportunities for work in Retford and the surrounding area and a corresponding surge of incoming workers. The town expanded as houses and public facilities were built for the increased working population and their families.

In 1878 East and West Retford were assimilated into a single borough, and Retford remains an important market town to this day.

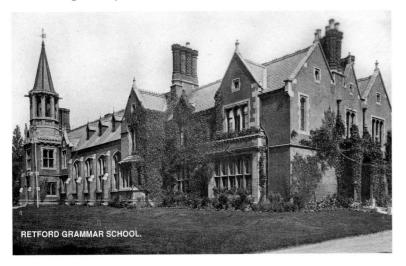

RETFORD GRAMMAR SCHOOL.

The town hall dominates the Market Square. The building facing the camera with the pediment and flagpole was Foljambe's bank, the first bank in Retford, dating from 1813. Its unusual name was derived from one of the original partners, Francis Thornagh Foljambe, who lived in an apartment above the banking hall. In 1863 Foljambe's became part of Becket's bank and later joined the Westminster group. They sold it to East Retford Borough Council for £7,250 in 1926, and the council remodelled it, adding a new frontage and reopening it as offices. The building on the near side of the town hall was the Half Moon Inn. Thompson, McKay and Co. Ltd., one of whose carts is in the foreground, acted as forwarding agents for the Great Central Railway Company from their premises at No. 2 Carolgate. This shop was subsequently taken over by Fletcher & Sons.

The Market Place saw numerous gatherings, some of them annual events and others one-offs. Each Lady Day young, unemployed people would gather outside Marshall & Sons premises, near the town hall, to offer themselves to local farmers as workers for the coming year. A group of suffragettes held a meeting calling for votes for women in the same location, using the back of a dray as a stage. Unfortunately some local men took exception to their message and grabbed the shafts of the dray, dragging the women round the Market Place amid a hail of ridicule.

This photograph was taken in the 1940s. The new town hall was constructed at a cost of £9,000 by local builder Thomas Hopkinson, and featured a tower containing a clock removed from the old town hall, which had stood at the entrance to Bridgegate close to the White Hart Inn. The Half Moon Inn, to the left of the town hall, was extensively remodelled in 1930. Two buildings beyond it lies the shop belonging to F. W. Woolworth's. Until 1928 the premises of Marshall & Sons, the town's leading grocers, had occupied this site. Woolworth's still trades from the same location today.

This Edwardian view of the Market Place on market day demonstrates how the stalls used to be set up much further towards Market Street than is the case today. The large, horse-drawn carriages in the foreground were a familiar sight at this time, both for transporting goods and people. Often their horses were taken to local stables while market business was conducted.

The Market Square is fronted by a number of Georgian buildings, although the town hall is Victorian in origin. An interesting feature of this Edwardian photograph is the signs on the buildings. The smaller one offers the residence to be let or sold while the larger sign on the adjoining building advises of alterations that are taking place, during which temporary facilities for the Nottingham and Notts. Bank can be found in Henry Spencer & Sons auction rooms next door.

V.6-3. *Retford War Memorial.*

Scrivens

The war memorial, made of Hopton stone, was erected on this prominent site in the square in 1921. Unveiled by the former MP for Bassetlaw, Sir Frederick Milner, the memorial listed the names of 302 local men who gave their lives in the First World War. After the 1939–1945 conflict a further 110 names were inscribed on the stone. The horse and dray beyond the memorial, standing in front of the white pedimented doorway, belonged to the Worksop and Retford Brewery Company.

VISIT OF THE "CHIEF SCOUT", RETFORD.

NO. 5.

EDGAR WELCHMAN
RETFORD AND WORKSOP.

Edgar Welchman has left a valuable legacy for those interested in the history of Retford. He came from nearby Gainsborough in 1905 and set up a photographic and picture framing business in the town, initially in Exchange Street and then more permanently in Grove Street. Welchman took a large number of high quality photographs of the area and its significant events, which he then turned into postcards and sold from his shop at 11 Grove Street. This example shows the founder of the Scouting movement and Chief Scout, Robert Baden Powell, when he paid a visit to Retford on 1 May 1921.

Market Place, Retford.

An impressive array of cars ranged around Retford war memorial. Parking was permitted in the square until it was pedestrianised in 1977. At the corner of the square, in front of the building with the hoardings around it, a stone horse trough can just be made out, a reminder that for many years horse power was a vital factor in trade within Retford. The photograph must have been taken prior to 1930 because it was not until that date that the old Clark's Dyeworks shop on Market Street (centre, with sunblinds open) was demolished and rebuilt along with its neighbouring shop. They became banking premises, originally occupied by the National Provincial Bank.

ROYAL VISIT TO RETFORD. 26/6/14. EDGAR

King George V and Queen Mary paid a visit to Nottinghamshire in June 1914. Whilst in the north of the county they stayed at Welbeck Abbey as guests of the Duke and Duchess of Portland. Their itinerary included a visit to Retford on 26 June when they processed through the streets to the delight of a large crowd.

ROYAL V  T  O RETFORD — INSPECTING GUARD — EDGAR WELCHMAN 27. RETFORD

Many special preparations were made for the visit of King George V and Queen Mary in 1914, amongst them the erection of a large canvas awning across the front of the town hall and adjoining buildings. The mayor, Edwin Swannack, welcomed the royal party and the King then inspected a guard of honour formed by the Sherwood Rangers.

The well-known local photographer, Edgar Welchman of Grove Street, took this photograph of Retford fire engine and crew in about 1946. For many years Retford's fire brigade was based in part of the town hall complex known as the Shambles, which was accessed from Exchange Street. From 1947 it became part of the County Fire Service, and July 1966 saw the opening of a purpose-built fire station in the town.

Looking from Market Street into Carolgate in Edwardian times. Although this formed part of the Great North Road it was a narrow thoroughfare, and at this time bicycles were a more common sight than motor vehicles. An interesting incident occurred on Carolgate in May 1911 when John Rutherford, a chauffeur, was caught speeding. He raced down the road at more than 18 m.p.h., sounding his horn. Since the speed limit was a more sedate 10 m.p.h. at the time he found himself before the magistrate and was fined. The shop of Herbert Dickinson, fishmonger and game dealer, is to the right while the premises of Fletcher & Sons (see page 2) are on the left.

On Monday–Wednesday 15–17 October 1923 the Picture House on Carolgate was showing Priscilla Dean in *Under Two Flags*. Admission charges were 5d., 8d., or 1/6d. For the rest of the week cinemagoers could watch 1920s' heart-throb, Rudolph Valentino, starring in *Beyond the Rocks*. As well as offering film shows the complex also included tea rooms and a billiard hall. By the early 1970s the Roxy, as it had become, was in a derelict state and was demolished to be replaced by a branch of Boots the Chemist, which moved from a smaller shop on Market Street.

The Pheasant Hotel was one of a number of hostelries on Carolgate built to cater both for locals and the steadily increasing passing trade. It belonged to the Worksop and Retford Brewery Company, who had their local head office in part of the premises. The hotel was demolished in the 1970s to be replaced by shops.

The Co-op shop on Carolgate was known as the Arcadia store. It was built on a site previously occupied by Dr J. C. Teasdale's house and gardens. When it opened in 1929 it was the height of modern design, but times and tastes change and less than fifty years later it was demolished to be replaced by a faceless, modern structure.

A mounted military group passing from Bridgegate towards Churchgate. In the background are the premises of F. Broadbery, poulterer and fish and game dealer. War was declared in August 1914 and a local force, the Sherwood Rangers Yeomanry, was mobilised and transferred to Norfolk on 11 August. Other men quickly joined up while those remaining at home aided the war effort in a variety of ways. For instance Babworth Hall was turned into an auxiliary military hospital. The First World War came briefly to Retford on 2 September 1916 when there was a Zeppelin raid, with bombs dropping to the east of the town close to the gasometers on Grove Street.

Although Carolgate was part of the Great North Road it was still essentially a quiet thoroughfare through a sleepy country town. Indeed the residents posing for the photographer on this early twentieth century postcard appear unconcerned at the prospect of a sudden rush of traffic. A sign to the right offers motorists petrol and car cleaning, although at this time Mrs Olive Backer at No. 50 is likely to have attracted more customers to her cycle agency than the garage opposite did.

East Retford Church.

Founded in the twelfth century, St Swithun's has experienced a chequered history, having been seriously damaged by fire in 1528 and by a gale in 1651. On both occasions major rebuilding was required. The Victorian era saw extensive renovations to the church which were completed in 1873. A vicarage was built during the same year and demolished in 1977. Note the position of the cannon in front of the church.

The bronze cannon in Cannon Square was one of many weapons captured from the Russian army by British soldiers at Sebastopol. A number of local men fought in the Crimean War and it was thought appropriate to install one of the cannons in Retford as a permanent memorial. The 1,000 lb gun was brought to the town by rail in April 1858 and a site outside the parish church was chosen as its new home. It is fortunate that it remains in position today, for when the national collection of metal began during the Second World War the cannon, along with the railings from around the grounds of St Swithun's Church, was collected and sent to Bradshaw's foundry for melting down. It is not known how the cannon escaped, but it was returned to its rightful place soon after the war. Another cannon came to Retford as a war trophy at the end of the First World War. Soldiers triumphantly pulled this through the streets of the town in front of cheering crowds and it was placed on display on waste ground near Carolgate bridge, where it remained until the mid-1920s when the land was used for the site of the Majestic cinema (opened in 1927).

Churchgate looking towards Bridgegate. Herbert Wilkinson lived at no. 13 Churchgate and was licensee of the Vine Inn (far right of picture). Beyond was the Public Benefit Boot Company and next to that Hildred's ironmongers.

W.6. CHAPEL GATE, RETFORD

AQJAY.

The Crown Hotel, seen here advertising locally-produced Worksop ales and Priorwell stout, was the main hostelry in Retford for many years. The original building had two gables facing the street and a thatched roof, and the replacement in the picture was erected in 1754. This had stabling for 40 horses, reflecting its original role as a coaching inn. The Crown proved very popular with locally-based servicemen during the Second World War, but went into decline afterwards. It eventually closed and in more recent times the building was converted into a branch of a building society, although it now stands empty and forlorn. Just a little further along the road is Ye Old Sun Inn, established in the 1750s and one of the oldest surviving buildings in Retford.

The railings on the left marked the boundary of the property belonging to local solicitor and former Mayor of Retford, H. T. Denman. In 1926 he made the generous gift of the house and land to Retford Corporation so that it could be converted into a museum and library. This opened in October 1927, and with extensions to cater for modern requirements the library still serves the citizens of Retford today.

Market Square, Retford.

G. 2833.

Behind the traffic island is the long-established shop of Fred Spencer, clothier, at 31 Market Street. Its neighbour is Bernard Neale, ironmonger, and a little further along is Cannon's café and the Wallpaper Stores. Market Street numbering commences on the other side of Churchgate with P. R. Rowell & Sons' drapers at no. 1. J. Pullar, dyers and cleaners of Perth, had a shop at no. 2, only three doors away from – and in direct competition to – local company Clark's of Retford.

The White Hart obtained its first licence in 1731 and would probably have remained a small, local inn if the Great North Road hadn't been re-routed past its front door in 1776. It quickly became a popular stopping point for stagecoaches. By the early nineteenth century at least eighteen stagecoaches called daily to change their horses and load and unload passengers and mail. The Dennett family took over the White Hart in 1818 and built up its trade over the following century. Northbound coaches would travel to York and onwards to Newcastle and Edinburgh, while to the south the service extended to London. Local coach tours around the Dukeries also set off from the White Hart.

The coming of the railways in 1849 meant a major decline in traffic on the Great North Road, and a number of hotels in Retford found their profits dwindling. A few went to the wall while others adapted to the changing situation. One such was the White Hart. Although it was some distance from the railway station it made sterling efforts to attract – and cater for – railway passengers by sending a carriage to meet each train. In the early years of the last century Reuben Hare was a well-known local character whose job was to drive the White Hart's four-wheeler, which ferried passengers and parcels between the station and the hotel.

BRIDGE GATE, RETFORD

G 2834

For many years Bridgegate formed part of the Great North Road through Retford. This is the section leading away from Market Street with the White Hart on the photographer's left. The presence of a gun shop, right, reflects Retford's position as the market town for a number of rural villages. Further along on the same side stood the shop of Chas. Butler, stationer, at no. 14. The telephone number for the shop was No. 4, suggesting that it was one of the first businesses in the town to have a phone. The shop also acted as the correspondent for, and the branch office of, the *Yorkshire Post*.

Continuing down Bridgegate and across the River Idle one reaches West Retford, originally a separate (and older) settlement from East Retford, with its own parish church, St Michael's. The community in East Retford grew faster than its more ancient neighbour due in no small part to the presence of the market and the influence of local religious institutions.

A tranquil scene on the River Idle, with rowing boats on hand and children enjoying fishing. The river was not always so calm, however, and the highest recorded flood occurred in 1797, lasting from Christmas Eve until February. This was so severe that after the river burst its banks parts of the Market Square were flooded to a depth of three feet. The power of the water was so strong that paving stones were torn up and in West Retford a grocery shop and part of a house were washed away. In normal circumstances the river had other uses apart from recreational ones. Many streets were paved with flint stones and became very dusty in summer, in spite of corporation water carts sprinkling water on them. On market days horses and drays would become hot and dirty and it was a tradition for the drivers, once they had conducted their business in the town, to ride up Bridgegate and down River Lane. They would then drive their vehicles down the gently sloping bank straight into the river for a wash.

The ivy-clad Newcastle Arms' location on Bridgegate meant that it attracted considerable passing trade from the Great North Road. It was particularly popular with carriers from outlying villages. The pub's name stems from its long association with the Dukes of Newcastle who lived at nearby Clumber House. During election times the Duke's supporters would set up their headquarters in the inn where copious amounts of free ale were distributed in an effort to secure votes.

200.46. North Rd. Retford.

J. L. Sneath had one of the earliest garages in the area, situated in a strategic position on the corner of Bridgegate and Hospital Road. Initially Mr Sneath dealt in bicycles too, but as cars gradually achieved a wider ownership he specialised in these. His wife ran a sweet and tobacconists shop from the same premises which probably explains the 'Teas' sign by the door.

Trinity Hospital is one of the most prominent charitable institutions in Retford, dating from 1615 when John Darrel died and left his home, Retford Old Hall, along with land and money, for the benefit of the poor of the parish. The Hospice of the Holy and Undivided was set up in Darrel's old home in West Retford, and there sixteen old men were looked after by a nurse and supervised by a board of governors. Gradually the fabric of Old Hall deteriorated prompting the governors to sell some land and build new accommodation. Architect Edward Blore, famous for designing Lambeth Palace, was employed to draw up plans and the new building was completed in 1833. It was not ideal, however, and in 1872 the central section was radically altered. Like its predecessor, the new building housed sixteen aged and deserving males of the parish who in return for agreeing to attend church regularly, not swear, blaspheme or get drunk were given accommodation, free coal, a weekly sum of cash and provided with a new cloak every two years.

Babworth Road, leading out of West Retford towards Worksop, presented a rural scene at the turn of the twentieth century. Today the detached houses on the left remain but have been joined by a long row of dwellings beyond them. To the right, in what were then fields, a new Babworth Road has been constructed making this old strip of road a cul-de-sac. The modern St Joseph's Catholic Church stands next to the new road today. Just discernible in the distance is the railway crossing passing over the road. A bridge now carries Babworth Road over the tracks.

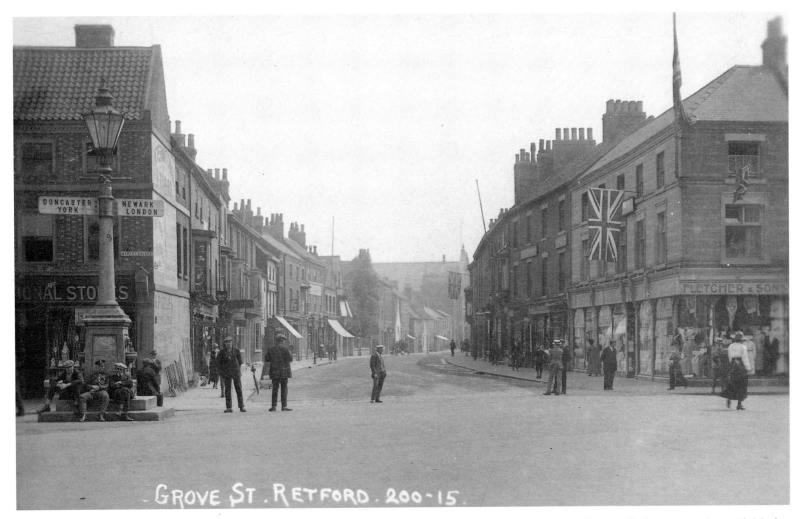

_GROVE ST. RETFORD. 200-15._

At the beginning of the 1920s Grove Street was flanked by Fletcher & Sons and the International Tea Company's Stores Ltd. at its junction with Market Street. The signpost in the foreground indicates that the Great North Road ran across this junction. Grove Street was traditionally the venue for Retford's horse fair, held in March each year. Horses and ponies were colourfully paraded up and down this wide thoroughfare to show them to their best advantage.

From humble beginnings Hezekiah Clark rose to have a profound influence on the town of Retford. In 1798, finding himself out of work and unable to find employment as a dyer, he decided to set up in business himself, operating a dyehouse at his home in Little Lane off Moorgate. Clark prospered and in 1854 his company was able to buy premises in Grove Street, where a laundry business was set up behind the shop. The company continued to grow, employing an increasing number of local people, and in the 1890s it was necessary to expand further to premises at Hallcroft. Clarks of Retford became known nationally and made a significant contribution to the economy of the town. The mosaic title 'Laundry', seen on the building to the left, still catches the eye as one walks down Grove Street today.

The Retford area has a strong Wesleyan tradition; indeed John Wesley paid a visit to the town in 1779 when he preached outside the old town hall. In 1823 a chapel was built in Grove Street, but even though it had seating for 600 it could not accommodate everyone who wanted to attend services. The chapel was replaced by this substantial structure, built on the same site in 1880 and costing £6,000. It had accommodation for 1,000. Edgar Welchman took the photograph of the chapel's organ.

RETFORD WESLEYAN CHURCH     EDGAR WELCHMAN RETFORD.

Retford Corporation were so pleased to receive parliamentary approval to route the Chesterfield Canal through their town to the Trent that they ordered the church bells of St Swithun's to be rung for four days in celebration. The first boat travelled from Worksop to Retford in 1774 and when the project was completed in 1777 it meant that the town had an east–west route for transporting goods to supplement the north–south route provided by the Great North Road. Prior to the First World War the Chesterfield Canal provided locals with one of the highlights of their year, when each August bank holiday a Mr Crossland ran barge trips from the town wharf to Wiseton. The goods barges would be cleaned up and fitted with seats, the horses would wear their full sets of brasses, polished for the occasion, and even the tow rope would be specially whitened. For many it would be their only trip out of Retford in the whole year.

Moorgate Hill, which led up to Welham bridge and the Hop Pole Inn, was an area of Retford that developed in the second half of the nineteenth century in order to provide accommodation for the town's rapidly increasing population. In 1918 it was possible to rent a house for 2/9d. a week in the Moorgate area of Retford.

200.44. Moor Gate. Retford.

Moorgate was very much a working class district and contained a number of public houses, including the Queen's Head Inn, seen here selling Hewitt's gold medal ales.

St Saviour's Church on Welham Road was built in 1828 to cater for the substantial rise in population in this part of town. It was constructed in white brick in the Gothic style and had seating for 900. In 1920 a war memorial was erected in the church to commemorate the 65 men of the parish who lost their lives in the First World War.

200.42 Queen's Street. Retford.

Queen Street, running between Station Road and Babworth Road, was developed in the middle of the nineteenth century when the arrival of the railways brought increased trade and prosperity to the town. Retford's population increased from 5,999 in 1831 to 12,340 in 1901. From 1849 onwards there was increased demand for housing on the western edge of the town close to the railway.

Queen's Hotel, Retford.
H. L. Dewick Propr.

*TEL 64*

Although Retford had many hotels and inns to cater for the needs of road and canal travellers, the coming of the railways in the early years of Queen Victoria's reign created a new demand. The railway station was sited on the edge of town and although carriages were laid on to ferry passengers to and from the established hostelries, many people preferred to stay close to the railway on which they were travelling. The Queen's Hotel was built adjacent to the railway, on Queen Street, to address this need.

The first railway to arrive in Retford was the Manchester, Sheffield and Lincolnshire line which opened on 16 July 1849. It used a station at Thrumpton. The Great Northern Company were not far behind, setting up their London to York service later the same year. They too initially used Thrumpton station, but being so far away from the centre of population this proved unsatisfactory and in 1852 a purpose-built station (illustrated here) was constructed on some spare land at the edge of Retford.

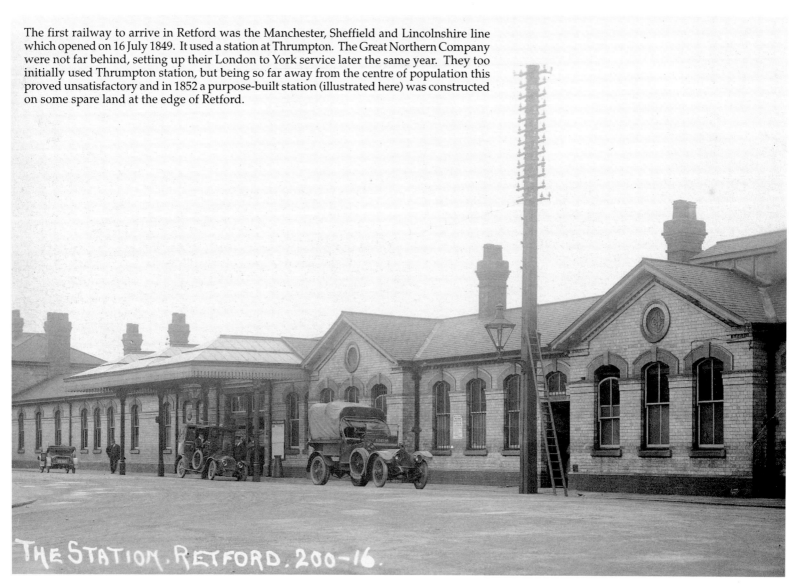

THE STATION. RETFORD. 200-16.

From the outset Retford station was a busy one, and it is not surprising therefore that occasional mishaps occurred on local lines. Two major accidents stand out. In August 1873, at the point where the Great Northern and Great Central lines crossed, a fish train crashed into a passenger train killing three people and injuring 40 others. Fifty years later on Tuesday 13 February 1923, this time about 300 yards north of the station, the Flying Scotsman express, travelling at 50–60 m.p.h. in fog, ran into the back of a stationary goods train. As it was only 5.05 a.m. most of the passengers were sleeping and escaped serious injury, but the driver, fireman and an inspector travelling on the footplate died of their injuries as the engine and first two carriages were derailed.

The Prince of Wales made a three day visit to north Nottinghamshire at the end of July 1923, staying with the Duke of Portland at Welbeck Abbey. As part of the visit he stopped off at Retford where he was met at the station by the Mayor, Alderman S. H. Clay, the Mayoress, the High Sheriff of Nottinghamshire, C. A. Longbotham and the Town Clerk. To commemorate his visit he was presented with an illuminated address. Afterwards he travelled to the Market Place where, accompanied by Major E. Milner, he inspected a gathering of ex-servicemen.

Queen Street, originally the main approach to the railway station, was the site of St Joseph's Catholic Church, which was built in 1895 on a site costing £400. The church was constructed out of iron and was known as the 'Tin Tabernacle'. It had accommodation for a congregation of 150.

Eventually the old St Joseph's was replaced by a new building on the nearby Babworth Road.

53602. J.V.

Early medical provision in Retford was poor, and in 1577 nearly half the population of 600 died of plague. By the time of Queen Victoria's reign there was a dispensary and small cottage hospital in Chapelgate. In 1894, as a result of private donations, White Hall on Thrumpton Lane (seen here) was purchased and turned into a cottage hospital with room for a dozen inpatients. The hospital was extended between 1900 and 1902, and in 1909 a dispensary was added. These facilities served the town until 1923 when Hercy Denman donated some land and a purpose-built hospital was opened.

With its wide, well surfaced carriageway flanked with trees, London Road was one of the most sought-after places to live in Retford. Other roads in the town were less well looked after, and a survey of 1881 described them as being in most instances little more than stony tracks. This prompted the corporation into action, and they purchased a steam roller to carry out much needed repairs. Motor car ownership was slow to take off in Retford. By 1903 there were only five vehicles registered in the town, although other vehicles, like this open topped car seen passing the Nags Head Inn on London Road, travelled through the town on the Great North Road.

GRAMMAR SCHOOL RETFORD.　　　44.　　　WELCHMAN RETFORD.

Retford Grammar School has a long history and can trace its origins to 1551 when it stood on Chapelgate by East Retford Parish Church. The school moved to these buildings on London Road, designed by Decimus Burton, in the 1850s. At the time it had facilities for 120 boys, 20 of whom could be accommodated in a boarding wing. It proved such a popular school that by the 1920s it had almost 200 pupils. This led to extensions in both 1926 and 1937, raising the capacity to 350.